The Positivity Tribe
In the Locker Room

Copyright © 2021
by Christopher J. Wirth / Fred Quartlebaum

MOTIVATION
CHAMPS
PUBLISHING

Printed and Electronic Versions
ISBN: 978-1-956353-00-6
(Christopher J. Wirth / Fred Quartlebaum)

To order additional copies or bulk order contact the
publisher, Motivation Champs Publishing.
www.motivationchamps.com

Praise for The Positivity Tribe in the Locker Room

"*The Positivity Tribe in the Locker Room* is a must read as it goes into depth about leadership, culture, teamwork and much, much more. Fred and Chris have once again produced a winner with this book."

—*Bill Self, Kansas Men's Basketball Head Coach, Naismith Memorial Basketball Hall of Famer*

———————

"*The Positivity Tribe in the Locker Room* is a great read. Chris and Fred take us through all of the ups and downs that every season presents to a team. They not only give us strategies to overcome these challenges, but they also show us how powerful positivity can be for a team, a coach, and a leader. And finally, you will find as you read about the journey this team takes that each of the lessons also apply to us as individuals and provides us lessons for our own growth and development."

—*Kevin Eastman, Former NBA Championship Coach, Current Speaker to Sports & Corporate Teams*

"A wonderful book that highlights the power of positivity. Pick up a copy for your locker room, company, or family. We do rise by lifting others up."

—*Mark Batterson, New York Times best-selling author of The Circle Maker, Lead Pastor of National Community Church*

"*The Positivity Tribe in the Locker Room* is a MUST read for anyone who wants to have long lasting success! If you are a player, coach, parent, or administrator, you will find yourself on many teams and what will keep you there is outlined in this insightful gem. We all need more Positivity, thank you for sharing it with us."

—*Tim O'Toole, Associate Head Basketball Coach, University of Pittsburgh*

"I love the idea of — We Rise By Lifting Others Up. As a professional basketball player, we rise and fall as a team. Culture is so important. If you are looking to improve your life, pick up a copy of *The Positivity Tribe in the Locker Room*, you will be glad you did."

—*Devontè Graham, Professional Basketball Player, New Orleans Pelicans*

"Make sure you bring *The Positivity Tribe* into your life. We can all positively impact one person, and this book will teach you how. Don't just read this book — implement it."

—Sviatoslav Mykhailiuk, Professional Basketball Player, Toronto Raptors

---

"*The Positivity Tribe in the Locker Room* is a quick and easy read. If you are a player, coach, parent or an administrator, this book is for you. Bring some positivity into your locker room today."

—Michael Locksley, Head Football Coach, University of Maryland

---

"Riveting, real, and raw from the very start. I found myself immersed in a myriad of feelings and emotions as I read deeper into the book. The lessons taught within showcase the passion stemming from real-life events, as outlined by the authors. This is a must read and riddled with a litany of valuable lessons."

—Al Hamed, MBA, MSM – CEO, Consultant & Coach

Christopher J. Wirth's Dedication:

I dedicate this book to my parents - Suzan and Ken. The two of you have always encouraged me and shown me true love throughout my entire life, no matter how many times I drove you crazy. I am so lucky to have you as my parents. Thank you for showing me what a real marriage is all about – love, trust, dedication, hard work, commitment, partnership and what it means to truly be a team. I love you both and thank you!

A.T. – Thank You! You have always had my back, and I am so grateful to have you in my tribe, in my corner, and on my bus. #WRBLOU

Fred Quartlebaum's Dedication:

For my sons Trey & Mayson- you've been the benefi-
ciary of many, if not all, of the lessons shared throughout the book. Thank you for trusting the process,
continue to be positive leaders in your college locker
rooms and beyond.

To all the players and coaches I've shared a locker
room with — remembering the locker room cele-
brations, the tough losses, and the special bond that
brought us together as we became more than a team
will always be a source of inspiration.

Foreword

I am honored to write the foreword for *The Positivity Tribe in the Locker Room*. This is an inspirational story about the ups and downs of a basketball team and how they overcame adversity to come together as one using the power of positivity. However, *The Positivity Tribe in the Locker Room* is really a story about a journey we have all taken or will take. My good friends Fred Quartlebaum and Chris Wirth go to great lengths to share with you the value of positivity in a world filled with adversity. Positivity is a decision. The decision of one person to choose positivity can make all the difference…to your family, to your team, to your business, to your community and to the world.

Take this journey with Fred and Chris as they outline a game plan for your life. A game plan on how to develop a winning attitude in spite of all the issues we face in the game of life.

The Positivity Tribe in the Locker Room is a must read for anyone and everyone. It will help make the world a better place!

Matt Doherty

Introduction

I first met Fred Quartlebaum in May of 2001. I had just graduated college, and I was in North Carolina coaching my sixteen-year-old boys' AAU basketball team.

I was the Head Coach of the Connecticut Flame, playing in the Bob Gibbons Tournament. Before one of our games played at the Dean Dome at The University of North Carolina, our team was stretching in the tunnel before the game. Matt Doherty, who was the Head Coach at The University of North Carolina, walked over to my father and me. He introduced himself, and we spoke for a few minutes. When he found out we were from Westchester County, New York, Matt called over one of his assistant coaches, Fred Quartlebaum. Fred, or as I call him Q, walked over and we had a wonderful conversation. At the conclusion, Q handed me his card and told me if I ever needed anything to give him a call.

The very next week I received my first collegiate coaching offer. I gave Coach Q a call. We spoke for over an hour, and I was very appreciative of Q's advice and time. I never could have imagined that twenty plus years later I would have the honor and privilege of calling Q one of my best friends today. In addition, if someone would have told me in May of 2001, that I would write a book alongside Q, I don't think I would have believed them.

Over these past twenty plus years, much has happened in our lives. There have been children, coaching positions, marriage, moves, divorce, new business opportunities, and a book. The one prevailing common theme has been our friendship.

When it comes to people that I respect, Fred Quartlebaum is at the top of the list. As a man, father, husband, son, coach, and friend, I have looked up to Q in many ways. He is a special guy, and a better friend. He constantly adds value to my life, by being one of the most positive people I know. I have witnessed Q win and lose games. His demeanor and approach have never wavered. Q has always looked at that glass as half-full.

I believe the true definition of friendship involves give and take. Being there for that person and having them there for you in time of need. Q and I have been there for each other over the last few decades.

When I was contemplating the idea of this book, I immediately thought of Q. I wasn't sure if he had the time or would be able to commit, but I don't think I would have taken no for an answer.

Before you begin the book, I would like to challenge our readers to think about the people in your own life. Think about the meaningful relationships you have now and look forward to the ones you will build in the future.

Aim big. Dream big. Value relationships and the defining people in your life. Do not forget the importance of positivity.

We hope this book inspires you, and encourages you with the Power of Positivity, and remember — "We Rise By Lifting Others Up."

Go For Your Greatness,
-*Christopher J. Wirth*

The Positivity Tribe
In the Locker Room

by Christopher J. Wirth & Fred Quartlebaum

Chapter 1
1st Game of The Season

"Let's go guys, hands in. Bruins on three. One, two, three!" Coach Jackson said to his team as they all put their hands together.

"BRUINS!" the team shouted back in unison before running out of the locker room toward the court.

As the pre-season number one ranked team in the country, the Westchester State Bruins had been anticipating the first game of the season since their very first practice six weeks ago. They were playing in the Community Bank Annual Tip-Off Tournament, which was held in New York City at the Madison Square Garden Arena.

Their first game would be tough. They were slated to take on number two-ranked Washington State. The number four and number five nationally ranked teams would play in the second game, South Dakota University and Pittsburgh State.

Surveying the historic arena for a moment, Coach Jackson turned to his assistant coach, Q, and asked,

"Do you think we are ready?"

Coach Q patted Coach Jackson on the back as they walked from the locker room toward the court. "We will soon find out."

Less than two hours later, the final buzzer sounded with Westchester State losing to Washington State 78–70.

The players and coaches walked to the locker room with their heads down, disappointed and dejected.

"Not much that I need to say right now gentlemen. Not how we wanted to begin our season, but tomorrow is another day. You know our 24–hour rule—we don't celebrate a win or lament a loss for more than 24–hours. Let's all keep our heads up. Hands in here. Bruins on three. One, two, three," coach Jackson said quietly.

"Bruins," the team mumbled softly.

Chapter 2
2nd Game of The Season – Consolation Game

"Okay gentlemen, the best way to put last night behind us is to go out and beat Pittsburgh State tonight. They are a good team, and they are very well coached. You can bet they will be ready to give us a good game. Let's play together like a team. Together on three," Coach Jackson said as he walked to the players.

The players stood and all put their hands in.

"One, two, three!" Coach said.

"TOGETHER!" the team shot back.

"It's time to go take care of business," Coach Jackson said as the team ran out to the court.

After a close and hard fought first half, the game slipped away from Westchester State in the second half. Multiple sloppy turnovers and bad shot selection led the way to a 14-point defeat, and their second consecutive loss to begin the season.

As the players and the coaches walked into the locker room to get changed, it was clear no one imagined the season would start this way for Westchester State. The uncomfortable silence spoke volumes.

Coach Jackson walked over to the coaching staff who were busy looking at the stats from the game.

Coach Q handed Coach Jackson a copy of the stats. Coach Jackson nodded as he accepted the sheet. "I'll see you guys on the bus," Coach Jackson said as he shuffled out of the locker room.

Chapter 3
Restaurant & Culture Question

Coach Q was having dinner with a long-time friend of his, Mike Jordan. They were enjoying both their conversation as well as their meal.

Mike abruptly stood when he saw another friend walking by. "Chris, what are you doing here?" he asked the passerby.

Chris turned and faced Mike. He seemed a bit shocked yet pleasantly surprised based on his smile. They gave each other a quick hug.

"Hey Mike. It's great to see you. I'm grabbing dinner with a client. How are you doing buddy?" Chris asked Mike.

"I'm good. I'd like to introduce you to a dear friend of mine, Coach Q," Mike said.

While extending his hand, Chris said, "Coach Q, from Westchester State, I am a big fan of your team."

Coach Q extended his hand as he smiled, "Great to meet you. We've had a rough start, but I believe we can right this ship."

"A strong belief is the best first step," Chris said.

"I definitely believe, but we need the team to buy in," Coach Q responded.

"Can I ask you a question, Coach?" Chris asked.

"Of course," Coach Q answered.

"How is the culture of your team?" Chris asked.

After pausing for a moment, Coach Q answered, "I am not a hundred percent sure."

Chris handed Q his card as he said, "If I can help in anyway coach, please do not hesitate to reach out."

After Chris was gone, Coach Q looked at the business card as Mike said, "He's one of the top mental performance coaches. I've really enjoyed working with him. He's had a significant impact on me both personally and professionally."

"I've heard good things about him. I might have to give him a call," Coach Q said as he slid the business card into his pocket.

Mike nodded in agreement and took a sip of his drink. "He has a very unique yet powerful approach in how he positively challenges his clients. I know he's doing a lot of work with various college teams. It might make sense to give him a call."

Coach Q nodded in agreement as he took a drink of his water. Mike could tell that Coach Q had a lot on his mind.

Chapter 4
The Next Morning Coach Q – In His Office

Coach Q was sitting at the desk in his office holding Chris's business card in his hand. He placed the card in front of him next to his phone. After a couple of minutes of staring at the business card he picked up his phone and dialed the number.

"Hello?" the voice on the other end of the phone answered.

"Hey Chris, this is Coach Q from Westchester State. How are you doing?" Coach Q asked.

"I'm good Coach, how about you?" Chris responded.

"What you asked me last night at the restaurant got me thinking. I was wondering if you might have time to grab a cup of coffee? I'd love to pick your brain about a couple of things," Coach Q asked.

"I'd like that, what does your schedule look like tomorrow or the day after?" Chris asked.

"Tomorrow is no good, but the day after I am wide open after practice at 2:30," Coach Q responded.

"Perfect. Let's do 3:00 at the coffee shop on Fordham Road," Chris said.

"Perfect, I'll see you then," Coach Q said.

"Looking forward to it. Go crush the rest of your day," Chris said as he hung up his phone.

Chapter 5
Coffee #1 – Culture is Built Over Time

Coach Q arrived at the coffee shop a couple of minutes early and spotted Chris sitting in the corner. Chris was reading a book with a chai tea and both his journal and pen in front of him on the table. Coach Q walked over, and their eyes met. Coach Q held up his own journal and winked as he said, "I never leave home without it."

"Me neither. It's great to see you coach," Chris said as he stood and shook hands with Coach Q.

They both sat down. Coach Q spoke first, "I've been thinking about your question from the other night."

"Culture," Chris replied, following Coach Q's train of thought. "The magical seven letter word that can turn a good company into a great company or transform a good team into a championship team," Chris responded.

"I love that, and that is definitely our goal. However,

starting off the season losing by eight points and following up that loss losing by fourteen the next night is not what we envisioned," Coach Q said.

"Remember, it's not where you start — it's where you finish. Have you thought more about your team's culture?" Chris asked.

"I have, but I am not sure where to begin. I know we have the potential to be great, but that word gets thrown around a lot in sports," Coach Q said confidently.

"That's true. I fundamentally believe that we all have potential, but the question is what we do with that potential," Chris said.

With a big smile on his face Coach Q said, "I know what I want us to do with that potential."

"I am sure you do, Coach. But there is a definitive difference between what we merely want, and the actions we are willing to take," Chris said.

"I told Coach Jackson that you and I were meeting today, and he was excited," Coach Q said.

"Coach Jackson is a fantastic coach, and I really respect what he has done with your program," Chris said. He handed Coach Q a laminated card. On the front side written at the top in big letters was the word CULTURE. Below, the word culture was spelled out with each letter representing a different word.

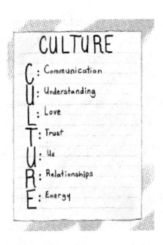

CULTURE

C : Communication
U : Understanding
L : Love
T : Trust
U : Us
R : Relationships
E : Energy

After Coach Q read the front side of the card, he flipped it over. On the back was the 7-Point Creed.

7 Point Creed

BE Kind
BE Positive
BE Grateful
BE Encouraging
BE Humble
BE Generous
BE Forgiving

Coach Q took a couple of minutes to look at the back side of the card, flipping it over several times to study it carefully. Chris could tell Coach Q was deep in thought. After about two minutes Coach Q turned toward Chris and said, "I really like this. My mind is going a million miles an hour. I am not sure if I am overstepping my boundaries, but could we possibly meet again?" Coach Q asked.

"I'd like that. What about the same time and place the week after next?" Chris asked.

"That works. Thank you," Coach Q said as he stood up to shake hands with Chris.

"Before you go coach, can I add one thing?" Chris asked.

"Of course," Coach Q quickly responded.

"I know being positive doesn't always come naturally to everyone, but right now it's going to be very important for both you and your team. The PMA, or Positive Mental Advantage, is something I teach. I have seen hundreds, if not thousands, of people and teams make slight adjustments that lead to significant results."

Coach Q was nodding his head as Chris continued, "Being positive in the locker room is crucial. It has to begin at the core of your program, and perhaps you can take ownership of it. As you look at the culture of your team, a positive attitude is essential to your program's success," Chris said.

"Hmm. I like that, perhaps something like The Positivity Tribe," Coach Q said.

"I like that. The Positivity Tribe in the locker room," Chris said with an affirming smile. "Now get out of here and go make it happen!"

"Perfect, I'll see you the week after next," Coach Q said as he walked out the door. Chris picked up his notebook as he began taking some notes.

Before Coach Q was about to start his car, he pulled out the card that Chris gave him to take another look. He stared at the word CULTURE and paused to think. He grabbed his notebook from the passenger seat and opened it. What Chris said to him about culture and a positive attitude really made him think, and Coach Q wanted to make sure he wrote them down so he wouldn't forget.

Chapter 6
Momentum – Games #3 and #4

After a rocky start to their season, Westchester State had a solid week of practice following their second loss. Having seven days off between their second and third game allowed the players to recharge a bit and gave the team time to make some needed adjustments. The last two practices Westchester State also began focusing on their next two opponents. The next two games were at home, which would be their first opportunity to play in front of their fans this season. The team was excited and ready to play.

The team's best player and leading scorer, sophomore Rex Smith, had become more vocal and was beginning to become the team's leader.

From the start of that third game, it was evident Westchester State was ready to play. They jumped out to a quick 12–0 lead before their opponent called their first timeout. The rest of that game continued to go downhill for their opponent as Westchester State cruised to an easy 25–point victory, with a final score of 82–57. Rex led the team with 31–points, 14 rebounds and three blocked shots, as he played a total of 34 minutes.

With a quick turnaround and their 4th game only 48 hours later, Coach Jackson decided to give the guys a break with a light shoot around the next day.

The following afternoon Coach Jackson walked onto the court and heard a ball bouncing. Coach was an hour and 15 minutes early for practice and found Rex working out by himself. Coach watched for a couple of minutes in silence as Rex finished off a tough work-out. Drenched in sweat, Rex walked to the free-throw line to shoot two foul shots. He made both of them. After the second shot Coach Jackson approached Rex who was a bit startled, as he did not know Coach was watching.

Coach Jackson asked, "How long have you been working out, Rex?"

"About an hour," Rex answered as he reached for his water bottle.

"I'm proud of you Rex, keep working hard," Coach Jackson said as he extended his hand to give Rex a pound.

"You got it Coach," Rex responded.

"I have to make some calls before practice, I'll see you in about an hour" Coach Jackson said as he walked to his office.

Coach Jackson stopped and turned around. "Hey Rex, games are not won on game days. Games are won in practice, in the weight room, and often when nobody is watching. Keep leading both on and off the court,"

Coach Jackson said while looking directly at Rex.

"You got it Coach," Rex responded as he sat on the floor to stretch before practice. He took another drink from his water bottle and grabbed his cell phone. He opened up the notes section on his iPhone and typed, "Games are not won on game days. Games are won in practice, in the weight room, and often when nobody is watching."

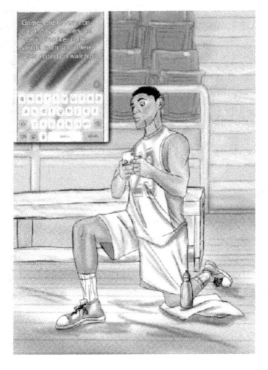

Rex took a couple of moments to think about what Coach Jackson had said. Rex picked up his stuff and headed to the locker room.

The fourth game began the same way the third game had — with Westchester State firing on all cylinders. They started the game on a 9–0 run when the other team's head coach quickly called a time-out to hopefully slow down Westchester State's obvious momentum.

The rest of the first half continued mostly in favor of Westchester State as they led 44–29 by the end of the first half. During halftime, Coach Jackson was pleased as he walked into the locker room to address the team. "Great job guys, way to control the tempo and keep rebounding the basketball. Rex, you are doing a fantastic job — but look for your shot when it's there," Coach Jackson said with enthusiasm. "There's not much I can say, but let's not get complacent in the second half. Basketball is a game of two halves, so let's make sure we finish strong. We don't have anyone in foul trouble, but let's anticipate them coming out aggressively to start the second half.

Team on three," Coach Jackson said. "One, two, three!"

"TEAM!" everyone yelled together before they headed out for the second half. As the team ran out of the locker room Rex stayed back for a minute to grab another drink of water. Out of the team's 44 first half-points, Rex made 22 points to go along with his 12 rebounds and seven assists.

Coach Q turned to Rex to give him a fist bump and a nod.

The second half started the same way the first half ended, with Westchester State once again controlling the tempo. With 16 minutes left in the half they were up 54–40 when the other team called for a time-out.

Rex continued the second half where he left off, as he tallied nine of his teams 12 points with three more rebounds, two blocks and another assist.

The rest of the second half continued to go in favor of Westchester State who led 67–49 with just over nine minutes to go in the game.

Two minutes later Westchester State had a two on one fast break. The point guard threw Rex an alley-oop that he caught as he proceeded to throw down a thunderous dunk, right over the outstretched arms of the defender. The referee blew his whistle and signaled a potential three-point play, and a foul on the defender. Right at that moment, Rex and the defender collided in the air on the way to the floor. Rex landed awkwardly on his left knee. Immediately, he winced in pain and rolled over onto his side. Two of his teammates quickly ran over to help Rex up before the trainer could run onto the court.

Rex gingerly stepped to the foul-line to shoot his one free-throw. Right before he received the ball from the referee, Rex looked over at Coach Jackson to signal that he would need a substitute after his free-throw. Rex dribbled three times, paused for a moment, and knocked down the shot. The buzzer immediately sounded, and Rex exited the game cautiously. The trainer met Rex at the scorer's table and escorted him into the training room.

The remaining nine minutes of the game were uneventful. The opponent made a late 8–0 run which drew the game a bit closer. The final score was an 83–61 victory for Westchester State, but the somber mood after the game told a different story.

After the game Coach Jackson addressed the team. "Guys, quiet down for a minute. The trainer is taking Rex to get his knee checked out. It looks like we won't know anything until tomorrow. Let's keep Rex in our thoughts and prayers. You guys played a very good game, and I am proud of you. I'll see you tomorrow." Coach Jackson quietly left the locker room to speak with the media.

Chapter 7
Stumble or Fall?

Coming off of back-to-back home victories, the West-chester State Bruins were playing well and picking up momentum with their overall record now standing at 2–2.

Coach Jackson walked onto the practice court as the team was finishing their warm-up with the strength and conditioning coach. He approached their team when they were seated and stretching at center court. The team looked up to give Coach Jackson their attention.

"I have some unfortunate news gentlemen. It looks like Rex tore his ACL. Looks like we'll be without him for the rest of the season."

After a couple of groans, and clear disappointment Coach Q stepped forward to address the team. "Guys, I know this is a tough loss. It is going to be very difficult to replace Rex, but this is an opportunity for us to all step up as a team. Let's remember that we are stronger together."

"Coach Q is right," Coach Jackson concurred. Let's do our job today, and let's have a good practice. We'll begin with our defensive transition drills" Coach Jackson said right before he blew his whistle.

Coach Jackson approached the coaching staff and handed each coach the practice plan for the day. He also nodded at each coach. That nod symbolized that they had a job to do. No words were spoken, but each coach knew the importance of what lied ahead.

Chapter 8
Coffee #2 – Adversity

Coach Q made sure to arrive early for his second meeting with Chris. When he walked into the coffee shop he looked over and saw Chris had, once again, beat him to the punch. Chris was sitting in the same seat with his journal and a pen next to him while he was reading a book. Coach Q nodded and made eye contact with Chris as he approached the counter to order his coffee. Chris was already drinking his chai tea.

With his coffee in hand, Coach Q approached the table and placed his coffee down and shook Chris's hand.

"What are you reading?" Coach Q asked.

Chris held up the cover so Coach Q could see the book as he said, "*Can't Hurt Me* by David Goggins."

"I haven't read it yet, but I've heard it's a great book," Coach Q said.

"It's a fantastic book. Mr. Goggins is quite a guy. He has this forty percent rule where he believes that when your mind is telling you that you are done, you are really only forty percent done. But enough about Mr. Goggins, that's not what you came to discuss. I am sorry about Rex, how is he doing, and how is the team?" Chris asked.

"Not good, he tore his left ACL and he's done for the season. Of course, we are going to miss him from the team's perspective, but last week I got a call from the top scout for the LA Clippers. He told me that the Clippers were planning on selecting Rex with the number five pick in this year's NBA Draft if he was still available," Coach Q said disappointedly.

"I know it's not what you want to hear right now, but adversity can make or break you – both as an individual, as well as a team," Chris said quietly.

Coach Q shook his head in agreement as he took a sip of his coffee.

"Have you ever heard the tale of the Oak and the Reed?" Chris asked Coach Q.

"I have. My father used to tell me his own version of the tale when I was little. What I can remember is the concept of bending versus breaking," Coach Q answered.

"That's correct. The main idea is while facing a difficult storm the mighty oak tree fights the wind and stands straight up and ultimately tumbles. The Reed, on the other hand, bends to withstand the wind and the storm, and doesn't break," Chris explained.

Coach Q quietly took in the comment and paused before he took a long sip of his coffee.

Chris continued, "Right now, your team is facing a storm, and the very simple question is how will your team respond. Will you bend, or will you break?"

"That is the million-dollar question," Coach Q replied with a bit of a smirk and sarcasm.

"Yes, it is," Chris said as he nodded his head.

"I know it's going to be important to continue to set the proper tone in practice today and moving forward. Any suggestions?" Coach Q asked.

"My first suggestions would be to sit down with Rex, one on one, and let him know that you are there for him. He is probably very disappointed, and I am sure there is a part of him that feels like he let down his team," Chris said.

"That's a good idea. I agree, and I appreciate the suggestion," Coach Q said.

"I would also express to him that just because he can't lead on the court doesn't mean that he can't be a leader. Challenge him to find his own positive ways to lead during practice and games, from the bench or sideline. When you connect with him one on one, perhaps discuss the idea of bending versus breaking. Although you and I have no idea what his NBA future will hold, we both know that he will be a man for the rest of his life. This is an opportunity for Rex to make the most out of this challenge," Chris said.

While looking down at his watch Coach Q realized he needed to head to practice. "I like that, and I appreciate your time once again. I am going to take what you said to heart, and I am going to try and make sure that we bend, and we don't break. Same time, two weeks from today?" Coach Q asked.

"You bet," Chris said.

Coach Q stood up and shook Chris's hand. Chris handed Coach Q a note and he placed it inside of his journal as he walked out of the coffee shop.

Chris sat back down and opened up his journal and proceeded to write.

Coach Q sat in silence in his car, thinking quietly.

He took the note out of his journal. When Coach Q opened the folded note, he found a quote from Andy Andrews. "Adversity is preparation for greatness."

Below the quote Chris had written something. "Coach Q – I believe in you, and I believe in your team. I hope this quote speaks to you, and perhaps you can use it to help motivate the team. Go for YOUR GREATNESS!"

Coach Q couldn't help but smile. He looked at the note one more time and placed it on the passenger seat. He turned on the car engine and headed to practice.

Chapter 9
Positivity Notes Appear

A couple of hours later, practice was over, and the players headed into the locker room. Taped to each players locker was a thin white "Positivity Note." The players looked around the locker room. They appeared to be confused, but also intrigued. One of the upper classmen removed his note and studied it. Written was a quote by the late great Kobe Bryant "Everything negative – pressure, challenges – are all an opportunity for me to rise."

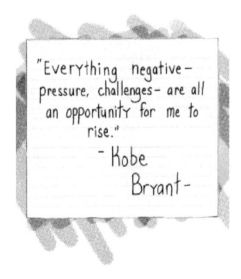

"Everything negative –
pressure, challenges – are all
an opportunity for me to
rise."

– Kobe
Bryant –

One of the other players grabbed his note and looked at the quote from Benjamin Franklin "Out of adversity, comes opportunity."

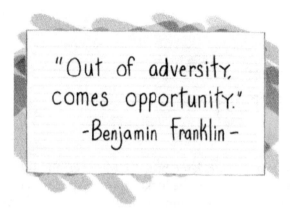

The rest of the team looked at their notes, and the players began to talk among themselves.

Coach Jackson and Coach Q walked into the coach's locker room together as two of the assistant coaches happened to be holding their own "Positivity Notes." Coach Jackson walked over to his locker to find his own "Positivity Note." Coach Q also has his own "Positivity Note" taped to his locker.

Coach Jackson smiled as his note has one of his all-time favorite quotes by Albert Einstein "In the middle of adversity, there is great opportunity."

> In the middle
> of adversity,
> there is great
> opportunity."
> -Albert Einstein-

Coach Jackson re-read the quote and then looked over at Coach Q, who is reading his note. Coach Q's note was by Henry Ford. "Coming together is a beginning, staying together is progress, and working together is success."

> Coming together is a
> beginning, staying
> together is progress,
> and working together
> is success."
> - Henry Ford -

The coaching staff stood in silence for a couple of minutes looking at their notes. Eventually, Coach Jackson broke the silence as he grabbed his keys and his cell phone from his locker. "I will see you guys tomorrow. Let's continue to work hard and grow as both a team and a staff."

The rest of the staff all nodded in unison.

Chapter 10
WE is Greater than ME

The next morning Coach Q was sitting in his office doing some work when he heard a knock at his door. Without looking up or breaking his concentration, Coach Q said, "Come in."

Rex walked in on his crutches. He looked dejected, but still managed a small smile as he gave Coach Q a pound. He asked, "Do you have a couple of minutes coach?"

"Of course," Coach Q remarked as he gestured for Rex to take a seat.

Rex placed his crutches to the side and he sat down across from Coach Q. "I've been struggling coach. I've felt really dejected, and part of me feels like I let the team down," Rex said quietly as he looked down at his hands.

"Hey Rex, look at me." Coach Q said. When Rex lifted his head, Coach Q continued. "Nobody thinks that. You were playing your best basketball of the season, and you were doing a fantastic job leading the team.

You made an incredible play, and unfortunately you and the defender got tangled up midair."

While looking at Coach Q, Rex said, "Thanks Coach, that means a lot. I just wish I could do more."

"Well maybe you can" Coach Q responded. "I know you've heard the saying *we is greater than me,*"

"Of course. Coach Jackson always talks about that," Rex responded. "But Coach, I have to be honest with you. Before the season I really wanted to be a top five NBA Draft pick. I still do, but right now, I want to help this team win a National Championship more. I'm just not sure how."

With a look of surprise on his face Coach Q slowly nodded and said, "Rex, I really appreciate your honesty."

"Thanks Coach," Rex said.

"The reality is that you won't be playing any more minutes for us this season, but there are other ways you can help us win," Coach Q said confidently.

"I'm all ears," Rex said with an intrigued look on his face.

"Right now, it is going to be crucial for us all to maintain a positive attitude both individually, as well as a team. One thing to remember is that We Rise By Lifting Others Up. There is also one other thing I think we all forget at times. From the very first time we ever play organized sports and put on our first uniform until the last time we wear one, the team's name is always on the front. With some teams our last name is on the back of the jersey, but the team's name is always on the front of every jersey. The front of our jerseys say Westchester State. Individually we are strong, but together we can be unstoppable. *We is always greater than me!* Why don't you carefully watch practice today, and objectively observe if you can identify a couple of different ways you think you'd be able to help lead us," Coach Q suggested.

"Deal. I can do that," Rex said.

"Great," Coach Q said as he stood and handed Rex his crutches. "I'm proud of you. The team could really use some positive support not only right now, but throughout the rest of the season. Often times, it's that little Positive Mental Advantage that can make a huge difference. It's going to be a challenging road if we are going to fight for a National Championship."

Coach Q pats Rex on his back in both a loving and supportive way. Coach Q nodded as he quietly repeated, "I'm proud of you Rex."

With a smile, Rex said, "Thanks Coach."

Coach Q quickly turned around to grab something on his desk. "Hey Rex," Coach Q said, "before you leave, I wanted to give you this." Coach Q handed Rex a "Positivity Note" and smiled as he got back to work.

Rex held the note in his hand and read it a couple of times. The note said, "Fall Down Seven Times, Get Back Up Eight" – Japanese Proverb.

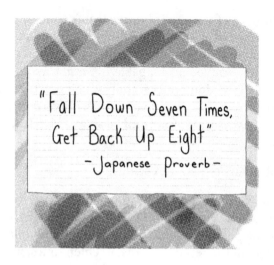

Rex put the note in his pocket as he walked out of the office. His mind was fixated on the various ways he could still help the team. Although he was disappointed that he wouldn't be able to play any more minutes this season, Rex was determined to give his best effort to help this team win a championship.

Chapter 11

Community Service – Local Soup Kitchen

For the last ten seasons Coach Jackson and the Westchester State Bruins served lunch down at the local soup kitchen. This season they were visiting the soup kitchen on the second Saturday afternoon in January.

About an hour after practice the players and the coaching staff were busy getting everything ready to serve lunch. For some of the players this was a completely new experience, but for the upper classmen and returning coaching staff this was something they always look forward to.

Over the next two and a half hours men, women, and children of all ages were served a warm meal by the players and staff. It was pretty evident, just by watching, that everyone really enjoyed giving back to their community. After the meal was served, the players went in the back to begin distributing the "goodie" bags they prepared each year. This year each bag included two buttered rolls, four waters, three cookies, and soup and crackers. In addition, each bag also contained a Westchester State Sweatsuit, two pairs of socks and a personalized "Positivity Note."

The "Positivity Note" was a new addition this year, but it was something that both the players and the coaching staff were extremely proud of. Each note was carefully written with the hope of inspiring each person to maintain a positive attitude and never quit.

After the players and staff finished cleaning up, they headed outside to their vehicles to go back to campus. Four of the players that drove together hopped into Kenny's Chevy Tahoe. After about three minutes of silence, one of the passengers, Brian, finally spoke "That really hit me. Even though I am just a freshman; I could see how much they really appreciated a warm meal, as well as their goodie bags."

Kenny said, "This is my fourth year volunteering, and each year it really leaves an impression on me. It helps me to take a few minutes to reflect and appreciate everything that I do have and the importance of serving others."

Brian responded, "Definitely. When I get back to my dorm, I am going to call my parents, as well as my girlfriend, to let them know how grateful I am, and how much I appreciate them. I'm going to talk to my family and friends about starting something like this in our community."

"That's awesome," Kenny responded. "We definitely have a lot to be grateful for."

"Oh, and by the way, thanks for driving. I probably don't say it all the time, but honestly I appreciate you driving me around as much as you have this year," Brian said sincerely.

The other two passengers also chirped up right at that moment to say "Thank You" to Kenny in unison.

Kenny smiled at their synchronized thanks and nodded as he turned up the radio. Although nobody said anything for the rest of the ride, their silence meant a lot. Everyone was definitely more grateful that afternoon than they were before heading over to the shelter. Kenny was thinking about how gratitude was an important part of life, and he made a mental note to be more appreciative moving forward.

Chapter 12
Make the Next Play

Practice on Monday started off in its traditional fashion.

In preparation for their upcoming game that weekend, Coach Jackson briefly addressed the team. "Gentlemen, if we want to play well on Saturday it starts with today's practice. Let's work hard and have a productive practice. We'll begin with our offensive and defensive transition drills." Coach Jackson blew his whistle which signaled that it was time to get to work. The players jogged over to the baseline to begin practice.

Ten minutes later practice was beginning to get sloppy. Coach Q looked over to Coach Jackson who was shaking his head. Two freshmen on the white team allowed a defender to drive right past them for a wide-open slam-dunk. They both looked at each other and casually shrugged their shoulders. On back-to-back possessions Brian took a really bad shot and missed, and then Kenny threw a bad pass that turned into a lay-up for the other team.

Coach Jackson had enough and blew his whistle. "Hey

guys, please bring it in," Coach Jackson said waiting for the team to all jog over.

"Gentlemen, basketball is a very fast-paced game. In a college basketball game, each team averages between sixty to eighty possessions per game. It's not about being perfect, it's about being consistent. It is so important to make that next play. Let's look at baseball for a second. A right fielder might only get one ball hit to him in an entire nine inning game. If the right fielder makes a mistake in the second inning, he might not get another opportunity for the rest of the game. However, in basketball, a player might touch the ball on offense twenty to thirty times every single game. Think about that. I don't want to encourage bad shots or sloppy passes, but we need to begin thinking about making that next play," Coach said.

The players were nodding their heads in agreement, so Coach Jackson continued. "For example, if you miss a bad shot Brian, don't hang your head or mope – get back on defense. Kenny, if you make a bad pass that results in a turnover, don't let it result in two more bad passes. Focus on making a better pass next time."

At that moment Coach Q stepped forward. "Guys, with a show of hands, how many of you are either business or economics majors?" Nine of the players hands went up. "Think about this in the real world for a minute. If you guys are in sales at some point in your career, do you think you are going to make every single sale? Of course not. But what do you do when you don't get a sale at your 1:00 p.m. meeting yet you still have another sales meeting at 3:00 pm? Do you hang your head and only focus on not making that sale at

1:00 p.m., or do you instead prepare and focus on your next meeting at 3:00 p.m.?" Coach Q asked.

The players were nodding in approval. Coach Jackson nodded his head, appreciating what Coach Q shared.

"For the rest of the season, let's focus on adapting that 'next play' mentality," Coach Jackson suggested. "Let's focus on being ready for that next play, and when it comes let's take advantage of it. We've got 45 minutes left in today's practice, let's focus on making that next play."

Rex had been watching practice from the sidelines, and he hadn't said much, but he felt now was a good time. "Come on guys, let's stay focused. Remember as Coach always said – it's not how you start, but it's how you finish. Let's finish today's practice on a positive note and make the next play," Rex bellowed demonstratively.

Coach Jackson looked over at Coach Q who returned the look as they both smiled and nodded their heads. Practice finished on a positive note with the players focused and attentive.

Chapter 13
Coffee #3 –
Pound the Stone Consistently

The next morning Coach Q was eagerly anticipating another meeting with Chris. As Chris had beat him to the coffee shop their first two meetings, Coach Q made a conscious effort to arrive ten minutes early this morning. When Coach Q arrived at the coffee shop early, he was excitedly anticipating that he would be the first one to arrive. He opened the door and looked over to what he had thought would be their empty table. However, Chris was already sitting at the table reading. Their eyes met as Coach Q pointed to the counter, signaling if Chris would like anything. Chris grabbed his chai tea and smiled at Coach Q. Coach Q smiled back as he approached the counter. He ordered his coffee and walked over to the table.

When Coach Q approached the table with his coffee Chris stood up and they shook hands. They both sat down as Coach Q asked, "What are you reading?"

While picking up the book to show Coach Q, Chris said "*Pound The Stone* by Joshua Medcalf."

"Another book to add to my list," Coach Q said with a big smile on his face.

"It's excellent. It's my second time reading it. The whole concept of a stone cutter consistently pounding that stone is not only a metaphor for succeeding in basketball, but also in life," Chris said.

As Coach Q eagerly nods in agreement, Chris continued and asked "I would like to read you a quick section if that's ok?

"Of course," Coach Q answered as he opened up his notebook.

Chris picked up the book and turned to page thirteen. "When you face the choice between doing the hard thing or taking the easy way out… will you pound the stone? When you face the choice to tackle a challenge or run from it… will you pound the stone? When you face the choice to treat a person poorly or well in a tough situation… will you pound the stone? When you face the choice to keep showing up or to quit… will you pound the stone?" Chris finished. He closed the book and looked at Coach Q, who was jotting something down in his journal. Chris took a sip of his chai tea as he gave Coach Q time to finish writing.

> "When you face the choice between doing the hard thing or taking the easy way out...
>
> ## Will you pound the stone?
>
> When you face the choice to tackle a challenge or run from it...
>
> ## Will you pound the stone?
>
> When you face the choice to treat a person poorly or well in a tough situation...
>
> ## Will you pound the stone?
>
> When you face the choice to keep showing up or to quit...
>
> ## Will you pound the stone?

"That was powerful," Coach Q said while glancing down at his notes. He looked up at Chris and said, "I am definitely going to type that up for both myself and the team."

"I have re-read that one section many times," Chris said.

"I really appreciate you taking the time to read that to me," Coach Q said.

"My pleasure," Chris said. "With technology moving at such a rapid pace – phones, tablets, social media, various apps, audiobooks and even podcasts, I feel that so many people are truly forgetting about the power in books. These things are incredibly valuable."

"I agree, and during the busy basketball season I rarely find the time to read," Coach Q admitted.

"Coach, is it that you don't find the time, or perhaps you don't make the time?" Chris asked.

Coach Q thought for a couple of seconds in silence before he shook his head agreeing. "You are right, and moving forward I am going to make the time to read for at least fifteen minutes every single day. And with that in mind, I am going to get moving because I would like to quickly stop off at Barnes and Noble to grab a copy of *Pound The Stone*," Coach Q said confidently.

Chris smiled and said, "You definitely won't be disappointed. Also, when you have five minutes, please look up the 'Stonecutters Credo.'"

"Deal," Coach Q said as he shook hands with Chris.

"I look forward to our next meeting," Chris said.

"Me too, have a great rest of your day," Coach Q said with a smile as he walked out to his car. Typically Coach Q would sit in his car for a couple of minutes to take some notes, but he wanted to make sure he had time to get to the bookstore.

Coach Q pulled away with an enthusiastic and excited grin on his face.

Chapter 14

Positivity Notes Continue

It was the team's day off for the week. However, the day before, the team decided that they were all going to hit the weight room and get a lift in together. When the players walked into the locker room to change, each player was pleasantly surprised. Taped to each of their lockers were two "Positivity Notes." The two notes said, "Pound the Stone" and "Make the Next Play."

The players took a couple of minutes to study the notes. Nobody said anything, but the players knew that the notes had to mean something.

Rex broke the silence as he finished getting changed and said, "Let's go men — it's time to go pound the stone and take care of what we need to do in the weight room."

The players finished getting dressed and headed to the weight room to put in their work.

Chapter 15
Small Wins Lead to Huge Victories

The players were getting dressed the next day before practice. Written on the large whiteboard in huge bold red letters were the words; "SMALL WINS LEAD TO HUGE VICTORIES"

The players each took notice of the message and continued to get dressed for practice. As Coach Jackson and Coach Q were always sharing life lessons, the players knew the message had to mean something.

A couple of minutes later Coach Jackson blew his whistle signaling when it was time to start practice. The players picked up the balls and jogged over to Coach and the rest of the staff.

"Gentlemen — Coach Q has something he wants to share with the team before we begin practice today."

Coach Q cleared his throat. "Guys, have you heard of the Stonecutter's Credo?"

A couple of players looked at each other, it was pretty evident they had no idea what he was talking about.

Coach Q pulled out a piece of paper from his back pocket and said, "I want to share something with you." He paced as he talked. "When nothing seems to help, I go and look at a stonecutter hammering away at his rock, perhaps a hundred times without as much as a crack showing in it. Yet at the hundred and first blow it will split in two, and I know it was not that blow that did it, but all that had gone before. - *Jacob Riis*"

> "When nothing seems to help,
> I go and look at a stonecutter
> hammering away at his rock,
> perhaps a hundred times
> without as much as a crack
> showing in it. Yet at the
> hundred and first blow it will
> split in two, and I know it
> was not that blow that did it,
> but all that had gone before."
>   —Jacob Riis—

Coach Q let that sink in for a minute before he continued. "It wasn't just that hundred and first blow that split the stone, it was that hundred and first blow in addition to the hundred blows that came before. A National Championship is never won during the first practice of the season. It's won consistently throughout the season, day in, and day out. A championship is won in practice. It's won in the weight room, and it's won when nobody is watching, through consistent hard work. I'm going to put this credo up in the locker room, and hopefully it can be a positive inspiration for us throughout the rest of our season," Coach Q said with enthusiasm and spirit.

Coach Jackson had been proudly watching Coach Q,

and he was impressed at how intently the players were listening. He smiled and said with some spirit of his own, "Okay men, now let's go take care of business, and let's win today's practice and pound the stone!"

Coach Jackson blew his whistle again, and the players jumped into action to begin their warmup drills. He had a feeling practice was going to be a good one.

Chapter 16
Los Angeles Clippers Head Scout

The next afternoon, Coach Jackson walked into the locker room holding some papers in his hand. The players were all seated in front of their lockers. The other coaches were standing off to the side.

"Good afternoon, gentlemen. I just got off of the phone with Greg Butler, who happens to be the top scout for the Los Angeles Clippers. We had a very nice conversation. Greg was inquiring about a couple of our players. He asked me six questions. Would anyone like to take a stab at what those questions were?" Coach Jackson asked.

A couple of players shout;

"Can he score?"

"Does he play defense?"

"Is he a good shooter?"

"Does he listen?"

Coach Jackson took a look down at his notes and said,

"Those are not bad guesses, but I'm going to read the six questions Greg asked me." Coach Jackson flipped a page and began to read. "Is he a good teammate? What is he like off of the court? Does he go to class? Does he have a Positive attitude? Does he LIKE or LOVE the game? Would you want him to date your daughter?"

Coach Jackson paused and looked up at the players. "Think about that for a second, gentlemen. As we often discuss, the little things *do* matter. The little things that don't show up in the box score often make all the difference. Small wins lead to huge victories. Finish getting dressed, I'll see you out at practice."

Coach Jackson put the papers in his back pocket and smiled at Coach Q as he walked out of the locker room.

Chapter 17
Coffee #4 –
Adding Value to Others

Coach Q walked into the coffee shop right on time to find Chris, once again, already sitting in his usual spot. He was writing in his journal when Coach Q approached the table. Chris immediately stood up and gave Coach Q a hug.

"Good morning Coach, how are you doing?" Chris asked.

"I am doing pretty good, how about you?" Coach Q responded.

"Fantastic, today is going to be a great day," Chris said.

Motioning to Chris's journal, Coach Q said, "If you don't mind me asking, what are you working on?"

Looking down at his notes, Chris said, "I am preparing for a presentation I am delivering next week to a group of college coaches."

"What's the topic?" Coach Q asked with interest.

"I have been asked to speak about the idea of *we is greater than me*," Chris responded.

"Interesting," Coach Q said. "How are you going to tackle that?"

"Before I answer your question, Coach, in three sentences or less, how would you address it?" Chris asked.

"Hmm. Let me think for a second." After giving the idea some thought, Coach Q said, "*We is greater than me* is all about adding value to others. Putting other people's needs first. Putting the team before the individual. What do you think?"

"I am not sure I agree or disagree," Chris responded.

"If that's not the most middle of the road answer, I am not sure what is," Coach Q said with a large grin on his face.

"Well, let me tell you how I am going to begin my presentation," Chris said as he turned his journal to face Coach Q. Written at the top of the page is a famous quote by John Wooden.

"It is amazing how much can be accomplished if no one cares who gets the credit." — John Wooden

"Coach Wooden was a huge mentor of mine. I had the opportunity a few years before he passed to spend an unforgettable evening with Coach Wooden and my parents. I am going to begin my presentation with that quote in big red letters up on the screen," Chris said.

"I have to admit, I am a huge fan of Coach Wooden, but I don't think I have ever seen that quote," Coach Q said.

"Or perhaps you have seen it, but you were at a different point in your life," Chris said with a half-smile.

"What do you mean?" Coach Q asked.

"I am sure your parents or grandparents had an

old-fashioned radio with a tuning dial. Those radios had to be tuned to the exact station or else you could not hear anything other than fuzz and static. Human beings are just like that. If we are not tuned into a certain channel and open to learning, we miss things. It can be a quote, music lyrics or even something somebody said. Part of growth is being open to other people and things, and always being willing to stretch outside of your comfort zone."

Coach Q was listening intently.

Chris continued, "Coach, I know you have to get going, but before you do — I would like to pose a challenge to you. Think about how you might be able to discuss the idea of *we is greater than me*, or perhaps share that John Wooden quote with your team," Chris said in a challenging way.

While standing up and shaking hands Coach Q said, "Challenge accepted."

"Great, I look forward to our next meeting," Chris said.

When Coach Q got to his car, he grabbed his journal. He began vigorously taking notes. He quickly looked down at his watch and realized he had to go. He placed his journal on the passenger seat and drove off to campus.

Chapter 18
Two Losses in a Row

With five seconds to go and trailing by one point, Westchester State had the chance to win the game. The referee handed the ball to freshman guard, Kenny Bird, who immediately looked to inbound the ball. Sophomore guard, Scottie Bryant, came off of a screen and caught the ball four feet behind the three-point line. Scottie made a shot fake and took two powerful dribbles toward the basket. After the second dribble he squared up and shot a wide-open jump-shot. The ball flew through the air. Almost immediately, the final buzzer sounded. The ball rattled around the rim before it fell off to the side. A miss.

Westchester State lost by one point. The home crowd let out a loud sigh. The players could feel both the air and excitement leave the building. Scottie immediately put both hands on his head and crouched down, a dejected look on his face. Almost immediately, three of his teammates sprint over to lift him up. The team walked off the court together trudging to the locker room.

Coach Jackson opened the door to the locker room and walked right over to Scottie. Coach Jackson took his hand and physically placed it on the bottom of Scottie's chin to lift it up. Coach Jackson put his hand on Scottie's shoulder in a comforting and uplifting way and said, "Guys listen up. The next time we get a chance to draw up a last second shot, Scottie is not only going to take it, but he's going to knock it down." Coach Jackson paused for a moment and extended his hand to give Scottie a pound.

Scottie extends his fist in return to coach, and the two of them both nod.

Coach Jackson continued, "I know this is not how we wanted tonight's game to end, nor did we want to lose our second game in a row. However, we have a choice to make, and the only way to make it is as a team."

Coach Jackson walked over to the whiteboard and grabbed a red marker. In giant letters he wrote; "WE RISE BY LIFTING OTHERS UP."

The players and coaching staff were quietly looking up at the whiteboard and what coach wrote. Coach Jackson paused for a couple of moments to let both the players and his staff reflect on the statement.

"Gentlemen — obstacles can often bring out the best in both people and teams. I challenge each and every one of us to take this moment in. Remember our 24 hour rule we learned from the great NFL Superstar, Emmitt Smith;"

"We only have 24 hours to celebrate a win or lament a loss."

"Take a couple of moments to look at the whiteboard, and let's all come back tomorrow ready to go," Coach Jackson said before walking out of the locker room.

Chapter 19

"Toughness" –
Jay Bilas & Energy Points

At practice the next day, Coach Q walked into the locker room holding a book in his hand. After greeting everyone, Coach Q moved to the middle of the room to address the team.

"Gentlemen — listen up. I just finished reading *Toughness* by Jay Bilas and I really enjoyed it. It made me think a bit about our team. Toughness is not gloatingly pounding your chest after you make a good play. Toughness is not flexing your muscles after you block a shot. Toughness consists of diving for that loose ball, drawing a charge, or being the first person to help your teammate up." Coach Q paused for a moment to let that resonate with the team.

"I think as a team, we can work on both our toughness as well as our energy. I spoke to Coach Jackson and he is fully on board. Rex is also going to help. We are introducing what we are going to call our Energy Points." Coach Q said as Rex wrote "ENERGY POINTS" in big letters on the white board.

"These energy points are going to consist of all the things that don't show up in the box score but can be the difference in us losing or winning a game. Whether or not we win the National Championship," Coach Q said.

Rex began handing out a sheet to each player. "On this sheet you will find the energy points we will be tracking not only in practice, but also in games. Diving for a loose ball, drawing a charge, tipping, or deflecting passes, running over to help a teammate up, making that extra pass, and rebound attempts. These are all things that won't ever show up in the box-score, but they all matter. Now everyone bring it in here, Energy Points on three. One, two, three!" Coach Q said.

"ENERGY POINTS!" the team responded together with excitement.

"Now finish getting dressed, and let's pound the stone today. I'll see you on the court in ten minutes," Coach Q said as he walked out to the practice court.

Chapter 20

Winning Streak &
Staying Humble

It had been a good two weeks for Westchester State on the court. They were sporting a five-game winning streak, and their confidence seemed to be increasing. Although Coach Jackson would clearly prefer a five-game winning streak over the alternative, he did not want the team to get too cocky heading into their next game.

The day's practice began with the players working on their offensive sets. In one of the drills, sophomore guard, Johnny Gordon, hit three shots in a row. After he made the third shot, he held his hand up for about three or four seconds too long. This little celebration led to the man he was guarding getting a wide-open transition dunk.

Coach Jackson shook his head as his eyes met Johnny's. Coach Jackson said, "Come on Johnny. What good is it if you hit your jumper and then immediately give up a wide-open dunk?"

A couple of minutes later, Brian got a little too fancy and threw a behind the back pass that flew right out of bounds. Coach Q quickly pointed out, "Come on Brian, we don't need those showboat plays. Make the right pass, don't try to make that ESPN top ten play."

With a look of surprise and embarrassment on his face, Brian nodded to Coach Q as he ran back on defense.

Practice continued to lose both its luster and focus. Junior forward, Mark Batterson, caught the ball at the top of the key. Instead of passing to Kenny, who was wide-open in the corner, Mark decided to go one-on-one with his defender. After eight forced dribbles going nowhere, Mark ended up taking an off-balanced shot which turned out to be an air-ball.

Just as Rex shook his head Coach Jackson blew his whistle loudly as he said, "Come on guys, this is not how we play basketball. Bring it in here."

The players jogged over, as the coaching staff joined them in a semi-circle facing Coach Jackson.

"Winning five games in a row is a good thing, but that was never our goal. Why are we acting like we are done?" Coach Jackson asked.

Seeing an opportunity, Coach Q stepped forward. "May I, Coach?"

"Be my guest," Coach Jackson responded as he gestured for Coach Q to continue.

"We need to stay humble, but we need to stay hungry. We need to remain committed to each other. Yes, we are on a five-game winning streak, but so what? Our culture is not just about winning, and we can't get distracted. No side streets moving forward, we owe that to each other. We are not only a family, but we are also a team," Coach Q said with growing emotion.

Coach Jackson nodded his head as he moved closer to Coach Q. "Well said Coach Q. Winning is important, but it's not the only thing. We need to remain focused, and for the rest of the season let's try to limit our distractions both on and off the court. No side streets. We've got about half an hour left in practice, let's finish strong!"

Stepping forward, Rex decided to say something. "No side streets. The only way we can do this is together. Together on three. One, two, three!" Rex said powerfully.

"TOGETHER!" the team and coaching staff all said at the same time with emotion and pride.

Coach Jackson blew his whistle. "Let's go back to that last drill. Move the ball, and let's make that extra pass. Remember, it's those small things that make a big difference."

The players eagerly sprinted back to their spots to continue where they left off with a new purpose in their steps.

Chapter 21
Coaches Dinner

One of Coach Jackson's traditions for the past three seasons had been the Coaches Dinner before the start of the NCAA Tournament. This dinner was very special as it was only for the five coaches as well as the strength and conditioning coach. No players, spouses, staff, or family. This is one of the very few times where the coaches got together for two hours of uninterrupted time to truly enjoy each other's company. This was a special time away from the court, practice, and the stress and pressure of the games.

This year's dinner was once again held in the back private room at Merlino's Italian Restaurant. The coaches were having fun enjoying each other's company. They were laughing, smiling, and sharing stories and favorite moments from the season.

After dessert was served, Coach Jackson grabbed his glass and stood up to make a toast. "Gentlemen, may I please have your attention. I often get most of, if not all, the credit as the head coach of our program. But as each of you know that is neither fair nor accurate. I owe each of you a very special thank you. If it were not for your dedication, commitment, and your hard work — we would not be the program we are. Clearly, we have had our challenges this year, but I love each and every one of you. I am proud to not only call you my friends, but more importantly, you are my brothers. Please, let's raise our glasses," Coach Jackson said as each coach clinked glasses with each other.

Coach Q nodded to one of the busboys who walked out of the room. A minute later the busboy came back with a large bag in his hand. The busboy handed Coach Q the bag, and Coach Q walked to the front of the room. Coach Q said, "Coaches — I need your attention for two minutes, please. This season has been one of the most rewarding and challenging seasons I have had in my life and I have spent a great deal of time working on myself, both on and off the court. Each of you have helped me, inspired me, encouraged me, and supported me in more ways than you know. As a result, I have a little something for each of you."

Coach Q turned around. With the help of the busboy, they handed each coach a personalized frame. The frames said:

13 Things Successful Teams Do

1. They put the team before themselves.

2. They value every possession – both on offense and defense.

3. The team doesn't need to be best friends, but they do need a level of respect and trust both on and off the court.

4. They are both accountable and self-accountable.

5. They communicate and remain Positive.

6. They make the next play.

7. They always make the extra pass.

8. They value character and culture.

9. They pay attention to detail and are extremely disciplined.

10. They have very clear and specific team goals.

11. They sacrifice individually for the greater good of the team.

12. They value WE over ME.

13. Their preparation is second to none.

Each coach took a couple of minutes to admire their frames. Coach Jackson walked over to Coach Q and gave him a big hug. Coach Jackson said, "I love you

Coach, thank you."

"You got it Coach, and I love you too," Coach Q said in return. "I also had one larger frame made, and if it's okay with you I would like to ask one of our graduate assistants to put it up in the locker room tomorrow before practice."

Coach Jackson immediately responded, "Absolutely."

The rest of the evening went really well. The coaches continued to enjoy each other's company. This is the one night they put the pressures of basketball to the side and made time to be fully present in the moment.

Chapter 22
Best Practice of the Year

The next afternoon, practice went very well. The players were moving with energy, enthusiasm, and focus. They were playing together as a team, communicating well, and focusing on making the next play. The coaching staff were standing together watching practice with a look of pride on their faces. On back-to-back possessions, both teams made two extra passes, and on the last possession Brian dove for a loose ball and landed out of bounds. Almost at the exact moment he landed, Kenny sprinted over and helped Brian up.

"That's what I'm talking about gentlemen," Rex enthusiastically shouted from the other side of the court. Rex had really stepped into and flourished in his new role. Although he still wished he was helping on the court, he cherished the opportunity to positively lead and inspire from both the sidelines and the bench.

Coach Jackson decided that he wanted to end practice on a positive note. He blew his whistle and called everyone over. "Guys — great practice. We're going to end today's practice with those two great energy points from Kenny and Brian. I'm proud of you guys. You've got fifteen minutes for extra shooting or stretching, the women's team gets the court at 5:00 p.m. sharp. Bring your hands in, team on three. One, two, three!"

"TEAM!" everyone said with enthusiasm.

A couple of players broke off to get some extra shots in while others decided to get a good stretch in with the strength and conditioning coach. Coach Q took a moment to watch and appreciated the positive energy.

Rex caught Coach Q with a proud look on his face. Rex couldn't help but smile as he picked up a couple of water cups off of the floor and tossed them into the garbage.

Chapter 23
Players-Only Meeting

When practice was over, and everyone was heading into the locker room there was a neon green post-it note on the door that said, "Players-Only Meeting – 5:00 p.m. Sharp."

The players walked in to find Rex standing in the center of the locker room with a serious look on his face. He was standing right where the coaches typically address the team.

"Hey man, is everything okay?" Brian asked.

"Yes. If you guys can all grab a seat, please," Rex responded. With everyone's full attention he began. "I wanted to take a couple of minutes to address the team in private. When I hurt my knee early on in the season, I was really down and out. I was beginning to go down this woe is me rabbit hole, but I was fortunate to have a very candid conversation with Coach Q. He not only encouraged and supported me, but he challenged me. Right after I got hurt, I asked myself why this was happening to me." Rex paused for a minute to look at each of his teammates individually.

After he was sure he had made eye contact with each of them, he continued. "I now understand that this injury didn't happen to me, it happened *for* me. I still hope that I will get the opportunity to play in the NBA, but my number one goal right now is to help this team win the National Championship. We are stronger together, and I love each and every one of you. As I stand here, I need you all to know I am so proud of you," Rex said with tears in his eyes.

"We love you too man," Brian said. "And I know we might not say it, but you have helped lead the way with your positive attitude and approach every single day, practice and game. Thank you. You are a true leader, and an excellent teammate. You created The Positivity Tribe."

Rex interrupted, "You mean *we*, together *we* created The Positivity Tribe!"

Brian jumped up and said, "Yes!" He leaned in to give Rex a giant hug. The rest of the team all stood to join in and gave Rex an awkward, but fun, group hug.

"Positivity Tribe on three!" Rex yelled. "One, two, three."

"POSITIVITY TRIBE!" the whole team screamed together.

The team was laughing and smiling. There was really no better way to head into the NCAA Tournament.

Chapter 24
Final Coffee Right Before NCAA Tournament

Coach Q walked into the coffee shop and immediately walked over to greet Chris.

"You beat me again," Coach Q said with a smile.

"Maybe I sleep here," Chris joked while shaking hands and giving Coach Q a hug. "I am going to grab a chai tea, can I please treat you to your cup of coffee?" Chris asked.

"If you insist," Coach Q said while smiling.

Coach Q sat down and waited for Chris to return. Two minutes later, Chris came back to the table with two drinks.

"Thank you, now what's on the docket today?" Coach Q asked.

"Well since you have enough pressure on you heading into the NCAA Tournament, I figured today we could just enjoy each other's company," Chris said.

"I'd like that," Coach Q responded.

After about forty-five minutes of fun conversation, Coach Q stood up to excuse himself. "I need to grab something in my car, I'll be right back." Less than two minutes later Coach Q returned holding two large frames.

"Chris, for the past couple of months you have challenged me, encouraged me and supported me. With sincere gratitude and appreciation, I would like you to have these two special things." Coach Q handed Chris the two frames. The first frame is the "CULTURE" acronym that Chris shared with Coach Q at their very first meeting. The second frame contains "The 13 Things Successful Teams Do."

Chris gratefully accepted the two frames. He spent a couple of minutes admiring both of them. Chris turned to Coach Q, and with a tear in his eye said, "Thank You. This means a lot to me. However, I too have a little something for you." Chris took something out of his bag and handed it to Coach Q.

It was a hard cover copy of *Pound the Stone*. A bit shocked, Coach Q flipped open the cover to find an autograph from the author and the inscribed message;

"Coach Q – Keep Pounding the Stone! Remember, it's not the hundred and first blow, but it's that hundred and first blow in addition to the hundred prior blows that make all the difference. I have been proudly watching you this season. Good Luck in the Tournament – go for YOUR GREATNESS."

With tears in his eyes Coach Q looked right at Chris and said, "Thank You." He put the book down on the counter and the two men embraced in a hug. After their brief hug, Coach Q looked Chris right in the eye and said, "Thank you so much for everything."

"You are very welcome, Coach. The only request I ever make to anyone that I have mentored is that they please pay it forward to someone else," Chris said.

"One hundred percent, I got you," Coach Q said.

"I know we will speak again soon, but I also want to wish you good luck in the tournament. You guys are ready, and you have put in both the time and effort pounding that stone," Chris said with pride in his voice.

"I will speak with you soon Chris and thank you again," Coach Q said as he gave Chris one last hug.

"Nobody will be rooting for you more than I will, now get out there and make that next play," Chris said with a smile on his face and a tear in his eye.

Coach Q nodded in agreement and quietly walked out the door. Chris grabbed a napkin and wiped away a tear, as he sat back down and picked up his journal.

Chapter 25

National Championship Game - Madison Square Garden

After a long and grueling season, the Westchester State Bruins found themselves back at Madison Square Garden. They had made it to the National Championship Game against Washington State.

The players were sitting in front of their lockers dressed in their uniforms. The countdown clock signalled 23:42 until tip-off. Some of the players were wearing headphones and listening to music while other players were stretching and getting loose. The assistant coaches were reviewing some last-minute adjustments together. Coach Jackson walked into the locker room to address the team. "Gentlemen, please pay attention." He paused for a couple of seconds to make sure everyone is focused.

Coach Jackson continued, "Here we are men, back at Madison Square Garden. Once again, we find ourselves facing Washington State, except this time it is for the National Championship. I know we have all seen how the media has labeled this game as 'the revenge game', and our chance to get even with them. It is not about getting even with Washington State, this game is all about *us*. I am so darn proud of each and every one of you. We have had our share of challenges and struggles this season, but we never quit. There were many times when we clearly bent, but we never broke. Every single one of us has embodied the *we* over *me* philosophy, and *we* are ready. We are not the same team we were the last time we played Washington State, and I know we are ready. Win or lose tonight, I am so proud of this team. I am not only proud of you as basketball players on the court, but I am even more proud of the men you have become off the court. We are ready, and we is always greater than *me*. Now let's go out there and finish what we started. Bring it on, TEAM on three!" he said.

"Wait a second Coach, and I am sorry to interrupt," Rex said as he stood. "If it's okay with you, I'd like to take this one?"

"By all means, Rex," Coach Jackson said.

"Guys, there is nothing more that I wish right now than to be playing in this game tonight alongside you. Over these past three months I have learned so much. I have watched you guys play hard, dive for loose balls, and continue to work hard every single day in practice. We grew together as a team, and we are definitely stronger together. I love you guys, and I am so incredibly proud of each and every one of you. Now hands in. Together on three boys. One, two, three!" Rex said with pride as both the team and coaching staff all put their hands in.

"TOGETHER!" everyone screamed at the top of their

lungs. The players were high fiving each other, giving fist bumps, and a couple of guys were delivering chest bumps as they ran out of the locker room. The team was excited, but they were ready.

Rex was the last player to walk out of the locker room, but before he did, he took a look over in the direction of Coach Q who was staring at him, and with a very proud look he nodded at Rex and mouthed the words "I'm Proud of You." Rex returned Coach Q's nod and smiled as he walked out to the court.

Coach Jackson turned toward Coach Q and said, "Thank you. If it wasn't for you, I don't think we would be here tonight. I am so proud of you and the incredibly positive impact you have had on our entire team. I am extremely grateful for you, your friendship and how you continue to positively lead by example. You have become an excellent leader."

"*We* did this together. We rebuilt OUR culture. We rise by lifting others up." Coach Q said with a proud look on his face.

Coach Jackson looked at Q and asked, "Are we ready?"

Coach Q hesitated for a minute and reached into the inside left pocked of his suit jacket. He pulled out a Positivity Note and handed it to Coach Jackson.

Coach Q had a mischievous look on his face before he let out a giant smile.

Coach Jackson looked down at the Positivity Note which said, "We Rise By Lifting Others Up."

With a look of surprise on his face, Coach Jackson shook his head and smiled. He realized that all along, the entire season, it had been Coach Q orchestrating the Positivity Notes.

Coach Q extended his fist to Coach Jackson for a fist bump and proudly said, "We've been ready for this for a while."

Coach Jackson turned to Coach Q and returned his pound with a grateful and proud look as he said, "Now let's go take care of business."

Coach Q put his arm around Coach Jackson and Coach Jackson put his arm around Coach Q. They left the locker room together and headed toward the court.

The End.

Acknowledgements

First and foremost, we need to thank Dominick Domasky and Motivation Champs! Without your help, guidance, and friendship – this would not have been possible. As the famous Jim Rohn quote states, "You are the average of the five people you spend the most time with" – we are honored have you in our corner. Thank you Dom, we love and appreciate you.

We would also like to say a very special and heartfelt thank you to Laura Edgerly, Cody Sims, Bethany Votaw, and Lynn Wagner. It is an honor to work with you once again. WE is definitely greater than me, and without each of you and your expertise, this book would not have happened. Thank you.

About the Author
Christopher J. Wirth

Christopher J. Wirth is a professional speaker, author, coach, podcaster, and trainer. He is the founder and president of both No Quit Living and The Positivity Tribe. Christopher works with sports teams, individuals, schools, and corporations to help improve accountability, effectiveness, and efficiency through his process – "The Positive Mental Advantage." As one of the top Mental Performance Coaches, Christopher strives to inspire his clients to go for their greatness.

Christopher is the host of the No Quit Living Podcast, which has been rated as a top 50 Podcast on iTunes in three different categories: Business, Health, and Self-Help.

Christopher recently published his first book, *The Positivity Tribe*.

Christopher coached Basketball at the High School and Collegiate Levels. In addition, he coached an AAU Team that succeeded at the National Level.

Christopher graduated from Washington College with a BA in both Business Management and Drama. Christopher was also a member of both the Men's Basketball and Tennis teams.

Christopher has three children, Zachary, Emily, and Mason.

About the Author
Fred Quartlebaum

Fred Quartlebaum has a long resume of basketball coaching experience, which encompasses more than twenty-five years in the Division I college ranks. He is currently on the coaching staff at the University of Kansas and has had coaching stops at North Carolina, St. John's, and Notre Dame among others.

While at Kansas, Fred has been a part of six Big 12 regular-season championships, two Big 12 Tournament titles, three NCAA Championship Elite Eights and one Final Four in 2018.

During Fred's time at KU, he's had the honor to see more than 15 Jayhawks move on to the NBA, including Andrew Wiggins and Joel Embiid, the No. 1 and No. 3 overall selections in the 2014 NBA Draft and Josh Jackson, the 2017 No. 4 pick.

Fred played college basketball at Fordham University where he was a four-year letter winner from 1985-89. He helped the Rams to an NIT appearance in 1988 and was co-captain his senior season. Fred graduated with a degree in communications and is a member of Kappa Alpha Psi Fraternity, Inc.

Fred and his wife Christy have two sons, Trey, who is a guard at St. Francis Brooklyn, and Mayson, a forward at Kennesaw State.

Other Books by Christopher J. Wirth

Experience the "Power of Positivity!"

A story for anyone looking to implement a more positive attitude and approach in their life. Join us on this journey of turning life's challenges into positive opportunities. Positive energy is contagious, and this book will inspire you to pay it forward. In a world focused on negativity this book encourages us to fully embrace the idea that "WE Rise By Lifting Others Up." What if every single day we all tried to positively impact just one person?

Connect with the Positivity Tribe

To bring the Positivity Tribe to work with you, your team, school, or organization please visit: www.ThePositivityTribe.com

Topics discussed include, but are not limited to the following, accountability, culture, goal setting, mindset, leadership, sales, networking, time maximization. We tailor each of our programs and presentations to our client's specific needs. This includes coaching, keynotes, consulting, multiple day workshops, or annual contracts. For more information or booking details contact Chris@thepositivitytribe.com

We welcome the opportunity to work with you!

Three Key Takeaways

7 - POINT CREED

BE **KIND**
BE **POSITIVE**
BE **GRATEFUL**
BE **ENCOURAGING**
BE **HUMBLE**
BE **GENEROUS**
BE **FORGIVING**

CULTURE

COMMUNICATION
UNDERSTANDING
LOVE
TRUST
US
RELATIONSHIPS
ENERGY

13 Things Successful Teams Do

1. They put the team before themselves.

2. They value every possession – both on offense and defense.

3. The team doesn't need to be best friends, but they do need a level of respect and trust both on and off the court.

4. They are both accountable and self-accountable.

5. They communicate and remain Positive.

6. They make the next play.

7. They always make the extra pass.

8. They value character and culture.

9. They pay attention to detail and are extremely disciplined.

10. They have very clear and specific team goals.

11. They sacrifice individually for the greater good of the team.

12. They value WE over ME.

13. Their preparation is second to none.

If you are looking for any of our Positivity Tribe Merchandise: www.positivitytribemerch.com

If you are looking to receive our "Positivity Notes," or bulk book order, please visit: www.thepositivitytribe.com

Together let's all
spread some more
positivity –
one person at a time.

Remember –
WE Rise By
Lifting Others Up!

9 781956 353006